SRI LA[illegible] PUJA: POWERFUL SACRED MANTRAS & COMPLETE GUIDE TO RITUAL WORSHIP

Diwali Puja, Varalakshmi Vratha, Akshaya Tritya, Kojagari Puja, Gaja Lakshmi Puja

Santhi Sivakumar

Credits
Mantra Consultants : Shri Krishna Bhat, Shivakumar
Cover Design : Oxygen Media,canva
Cover Photo : Wikimedia
Book Design : Oxygen Media
Photos : Muruli (Pixabay),Wikimedia and Santhi Sivakumar

Salutations to Maa Lakshmi, Who is the Auspiciousness in all the auspicious and who fulfills all the Objectives of the Devotees.I salute you O Lakshmi, the Devi Who is the giver of refuge and with three Eyes
O MaaLakshmi, whose heart is full of mercy, who is worshipped throughout the three worlds and who is the giver of all fortune and the mother of Creation. All glories to you, o shelter of all living entities. O fulfiller of all desires, You are the Supreme Goddess

SRI SUKTHA(M)

CONTENTS

Title Page

Copyright

Epigraph

PranaAm

Puja Essentials 1

Step by step basics to do Puja or Worship 4

Mantra Chanting Rules 6

Goddess Lakshmi 8

Ashtalakshmi: Eight Forms Of Wealth 11

Associated Symbols & Iconography of Goddess Lakshmi 16

Pujas and Festival Celebration Dedicated To Maa Lakshmi (Mahalakshmi) 20

Powerful Sacred Mantras for Goddess Lakshmi (Puja) 24

Invocation to Lord Ganesh 25

Shanthi Mantra 26

Asana Puja	27
Deepa Puja	28
Gayatri Mantra for Pranayama	29
Sankalpa Mantra	30
Kalash(a) Puja	32
Ghanta Puja	33
Mahalakshmi Mantra	34
Lakshmi Beej(ah) Mantra	35
Lakshmi Gayatri Mantra	36
Five Powerful mantras of Maa Lakshmi that brings progress in your life	37
Sri Mahalakshmi Ashtakam	39
Kanakadhāra Stotram	42
Śrī Sūkta(m)	51
Mahalakshmi Aśhṭotara Sata Nāmāvaḻi	61
Prayer	70
ANNEXURE	71
THANKS	81

PRANAAM

Namaste,

According to ancient puranas, Maa Lak shmi (Lord Vishnu's wife) is the goddess of wealth, prosperity and fortune. She is bestower of power and sovereignty. Doing Lakshmi Puja (Lakshmi Pooja) is an important ritual worship performed by Hindus and Jains to resolve all financial issues, remove all obstacles and achieve success. If you can perform this home Pujas by following proper pro cedures, it's not only memorable but is also auspicious.

The ritual is to invite Goddess Lakshmi. Before starting the puja, devotees con sider it important to clean our home and decorate the puja place (where the Puja is being carried out). During a Puja, we often repeatedly chant 'sacred mantras', 'Shlokas' and 'stothras' that help us connect with God to make our mind peace ful. It is believed that worshiping Lakshmi and doing this puja properly will remove all kinds of sorrows and pain.

Sanskrit is an ancient language and still remains today without any changes and structural modification. The mantras in Sanskrit are endowed with powerful vibrations for which provides our nervous system with positive energy. This is the Power of Mantra Chanting.

I have put in a lot of effort and made many revisions to improve and compile this book. Now I'm happy to publish. Your valuable suggestion for improvement is Welcome.

May divine blessings of Goddess Lakshmi bestow on you and your family with good fortune, wealth and success.

Thanking You.

Santhi Sivakumar

PUJA ESSENTIALS

- God Ganesha (Ganapathi) idol or picture
- Goddess Mahalakshmi idol or picture

Puja Utensils

- Puja Lamp with oil or Ghee soaked Cotton Wicks
- Puja Bell

- Coppor Pot or Silver Pot or Stainless steel Vessel (Kalasha)
- Coppor or silver or metal Spoon
- Arati plate
- Small Cups
- Any Jewelry (a bangle or chain for use during the puja)
- Seat for worship (Mat,carpet)

Basic Puja Materials/Items

- Kumkum(a), Turmeric and cups to hold them
- Sandalwood or Sandalpaste
- Akshta - Uncooked Rice mixed with turmeric (using water) in a cup
- Incense sticks
- Champhor (Karpoor)
- Holy Water (Like Ganga Water) or fresh pure water (To be filled in Kalash)

- Rose Water
- Fresh Cloth (Preferably Red color garment)
- Fresh mango leaves, wash them before using Kalash
- Fresh Flowers to offer Deity
- Match Box
- Puja Mantra Book

Other Puja Necessaries

- Coconut
- Banana
- Nine Cereals (Nava Dhanya)
- A bowl of five things (honey, ghee, yogurt, sugar and milk)
- Paan (betal Leaves) with Supari (If available)
- Fruits
- Sweets
- Banna Leaf (To Offer All Prasad)
- Neivedhya Prasada (Fresh Cooked Food)

(Note: Even if you don't have some of the above mentioned items, don't worry! Pray whole heartedly, chant the mantras properly you will get the Goddess Lakshmi blessings)

STEP BY STEP BASICS TO DO PUJA OR WORSHIP

- ✓ Without taking Bath don't do any puja arrangements
- ✓ Swastik(a) symbol is drawn in home entrance to welcome Goddess Lakshmi
- ✓ Sit on a piece of cloth or mat facing North or East at puja room.
- ✓ First, you'll clean the place and idols (*abhisekha: Water is offered for symbolic bathing*) by sprinkling few drops of water.
- ✓ 'Shri' is drawn on the floor with the paste of turmeric and rice.
- ✓ Vastra : ("clothing"): Cloth may be wrapped around the image affixed to it
- ✓ Aabaran: The deity is decorated with ornaments
- ✓ Light the lamps and ensure that you are placing two lamps (Deepa) on both side (facing east -towards sun or another facing North- for a god).
- ✓ Light an incense stick.
- ✓ Light an small brass oil lamp in keep it on your arati plate. (Use sesame oil ,ghee or mustard oil).
- ✓ Pushpa : Offer flowers to God's idols or images. (One flower will also be sufficient)
- ✓ Do Salutation (Namaskar) with folded hands and closed eyes.

✓ Sit down for a minute or two to relax.
✓ Start Chanting Sacred Mantras
✓ Offer Naivedya Foods such as cooked rice, fruit, Dry grapes,sugar, and betel leaf are offered
✓ Puja should be always performed by facing towards East or North
✓ After completion of the puja or Dipa(aarti,) make three Circumambulation (parikrama/ Pradakshina) around the deity.
✓ Namaskara or pranama. The worshipper and family bow or prostrate themselves before the image to offer homage.
✓ Taking leave from Puja

Mantra/ Japa is best done using a strand of beaded mala known as Japa mala made of Rudraksha, red sandal, Tulsi or sphatik beads. Or use Gyan Mudra while chanting.

Remember The Following

- *Tulsi (Basil leaves) should not be offered to Lord Ganesha. Goddess Lakshmi should not be offered grass. This is especially recommended for Ganesha.*
- *Holywater(for kalash) should not be kept in any plastic, aluminum or iron vessels.*
- *You should never face your back towards the idols of Gods and Goddesses.*
- *Dont keep the flowers in hand and offer it to God. Place flowers on a plate and offer it with your fingers.*
- *Dont store sandal paste (chandan) in copper utensils.*
- *Strictly avoid Non-Vegetarian*

MANTRA CHANTING RULES

- ✓ Read and pronounce Mantra carefully before starting chant.
- ✓ Do not give a break or end to the process once you have started it.
- ✓ Chanting the mantra out loud or follow Upamsu Japa (The Upamsu Japa : whispering or humming if Mantra which cannot be heard by any one)
- ✓ Chanting should be done with a fixed posture with Gyan mudra to allow the complete effect of the sound energy.

- ✓ Chanting should not be done like singing, or like reading. It should not be muttered fast, each syllable should be properly uttered with the required stress and pronounced with clarity.
- ✓ Japa - the mantra should be chanted for the count (Use Japa Mala)
- ✓ Avoid activities like sneezing, yawning or spitting (as it shows disrespect or insult of God)

***

GODDESS LAKSHMI

The word 'Lakshmi' first mentioned in the Śrī Sūkta of the Rigveda. The name "Lakshmi" is derived from the Sanskrit word "Laksya"signifies 'aspire' (aim or goal). Lakshmi is a member of the Tridevi, the three main female deities. The Tridevi, Hindu Triple goddess comprising of Maa Lakshmi (wealth, consort of Vishnu) ,Maa Parvati (motherhood, consort of Shiva) and Maa Saraswati (wisdom, consort of Brahma).

Goddess Lakshmi is the bestower of power, wealth and prosperity. According to the Hindu Puranas, Mother Lakshmi (Shri) was the daughter of the sage Bhrigu and his wife Khyati. She is the consort of Vishnu, called MahaLakshmi. So if a person worship lord Vishnu also along with, they will be very soon blessed by mother Lakshmi.

Lakshmi is known to be very closely associated with the lotus, and her many epithets are connected to the flower. Her Four Arms & Four Hands signify her power to grant the four object of human pursuit, Dharma (Duty), Artha (Wealth), Kama (Pleasures of the flesh) and Moksha (Beatitude-supreme happiness). Goddess Lakshmi holds half blossomed Lotus on her Upper left hand, her Lower left hand carries golden pot overflowing with gold coins. Maa Lakshmi is in Abhaya Mudra on her Right lower hand (the mudra symbolizes dispelling of fear, protection and reassurance) and Lotus in the Right Upper Hand. Lakshmi is described as bestowing gold coins of prosperity and flanked by elephants signifying her royal power.

Representations of Lakshmi are also found in Jainism and in Buddhism. Lakshmi is worshipped daily in Hindu, Jain & Buddhist homes and many business houses as the Goddess of wealth. Whenever you wish to start something new, praying to Goddess Lakhmi will give you all the success.

ASHTALAKSHMI: EIGHT FORMS OF WEALTH

Goddess Lakshmi is worshipped in several forms. The most popular manifestations of Goddess Lakshmi are eight which are collectively known as 'AshtaLakshmi'. AshtaLakshmi preside over eight sources of wealth. They are Prosperity, fertility, fortune or luck, health, knowledge, strength, progeny and power.

Mahalakshmi Or Adi Lakshmi

The first Form of Lakshmi. She resides in Vaikuntha with Lord Mahavishnu , who is the principal deity of the Universes .She is depicted as four-armed, carrying a lotus and a white flag, other two arms in Abhaya mudra and varada mudra.

Dhana Lakshmi Or Aishwarya Lakshmi

Dhana or Aishwarya means wealth. The one who showers wealth of prosperity and fortune. Wealth comes in many forms Financial, Love, Peace, Health, Prosperity,Luck Virtue, Family relationships etc., She is six armed with red saree (garment) carries Amrita Kalash(a), a lotus and an arm in Abhaya mudra with gold coins falling from it.

Dhanya Lakshmi

Dhanya means grains .Goddess of Food & Nourishment, provider of Granary wealth. Dhanya Lakshmi is the one who eliminates hunger. She is depicted as eight-armed, in green garments, carrying two lotuses, paddy crop and sugarcane. Herr two hands in Abhaya mudra and Varada mudra

Gaja Lakshmi

Gajalakshmi meaning Lakshmi with Elephant,the one who gives Strength, Power of royalty and Animal Wealth. . She is also known as a daughter of the ocean. She is sitting on a full-bloomed lotus and also having two lotus in both hands with two elephants by her sides holding beautiful vessels. Her other two arms in Abhaya mudra and Varada mudra.

Santana Lakshmi

The fifth form of Goddess Lakshmi, is worshipped to be blessed with healthy progeny (offspring) and Wealth of Continuity. She is depicted as six armed, carrying two kalash(a), sword & Shield, a hand in Abhaya mudra and the other holding the child on her lap. Her sword & shield represents a mother's ability to even kill someone to save her child .

Dhairya Lakshmi Or Veera Lakshmi

This form of Maa Lakshmi grants the blessing of infinite courage and strength for overcoming difficulties in life. She is depicted as eight armed, in red saree, carrying a chakra, shankh, bow & arrow, trishul , other two hands in Abhaya mudra and Varada mudra. She is the one who took the avtar of Maa Durga .

Jaya Lakshmi Or Vijaya Lakshmi

Vijay or Jaya means Victory. The one gives victory over all sort of opposition (enemies) and also for conquering hurdles in order to accomplish success. She is described as eight-armed, in red saree, carrying the chakra, shankh, sword & shield, lotus, pasha, other two hands in Abhaya mudra and Varada mudra.

Vidya Lakshmi

Vidya is education .She is Wealth of Knowledge and Wisdom. This eighth form of Lakshmi is dressed in a white saree and has a resemblance to the goddess Saraswati. She holds all four vedas, a peacock feather as a pen, Vard mudra and Abhay mudra

According to ancient Puranas , the other incarnations of Goddess Lakshmi, which are also worshipped

Saubhagya Lakshmi/ Sowbhagya Lakshmi : *The one who blesses with good luck prosperity*

Rajya Lakshmi: *The one who gives Power and Property*

Vara Lakshmi: *The goddess who bestows boons*

Griha Lakshmi*: Griha means House. Goddess of* house's fortune.

Vaibhava Lakshmi: The Goddess of wealth & prosperity

Bhagya Lakshmi: The Goddess of fortune & wealth

Vishnupriya: *One who is the beloved of Vishnu*

Jaganmaatha : *Mother of the Universe*

Other names of Mother Lakshmi include: *Manushri, Chakrika, Kamalika, Aishwarya, Lalima,*

Kalyani, Nandika, Rujula, Vaishnavi, Samruddhi, Narayani, Bhargavi, Sridevi, Chanchala, Jalaja, Madhavi, Sujata, Shreya, Thirumagal ,etc.,

Ref *: Shri Mahalakshmi Ashtakam*

ASSOCIATED SYMBOLS & ICONOGRAPHY OF GODDESS LAKSHMI

Red Saree And Lotus Flower

Goddess Mahalakshmi delineate wearing a red saree (garment) and sitting on lotus. She is known to be very closely associated with the lotus, Lotus flower are considered sacred. Many of her epithets are connected to the Lotus : *Padma, Kamala, Padmapriya, Padmamukhi, Padmakshi, Padmahasta, Padmasundar, Padmamaladhara devi* eic.,

(Nothing pleases Goddess Lakshmi more than the offering of lotus flowers.)

Gold

Goddess of wealth and prosperity, Lakshmi is associated with the gold. She wears ornaments full of gold. Her complexion is golden, representing a boon-giver.

(During puja, you can decorate Goddess Lakshmi by using your gold ornaments)

Owl

One of the names of Goddess Lakshmi is 'Ulka-vahini', means the one who rides an owl. Her vahana (Vehicle) white owl represents royalties, penetrating sight and intelligence. In many countries, owl is considered a lucky charm.

Shri

Shri is one of the sacred symbols in Hinduism. Shri means Goddess Lakshmi. During all Lakshmi Pujas, 'Shri' is drawn on the floor with the paste of turmeric and rice (after grinding freshly), would bring wealth and prosperity at home.

Swastik(A)

The Swastik(a) symbol pleases Goddess Lakshmi. On the pujas of Lakshmi, Swastik(a) symbol is drawn in home entrance to welcome Goddess Lakshmi.

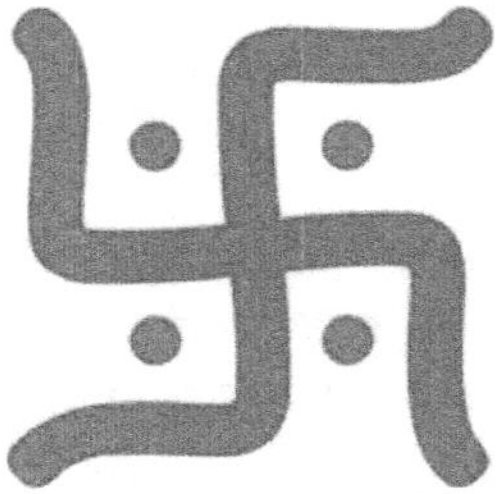

Shri Yantra

Sri Yantra, or Shri Chakra is a form of mystical diagram used in the Goddess Lakshmi worship. This most powerful yantra, is the symbol of the great divine mother principle, the source of all energy, power, and creativity.

(*E*nergised Copper *Sri Yantra* (Shri Chakra) are available at spiritual stores and online shopping portals. If copper yantra is not available, you can draw Shri Yantra (diagram) at your puja room)

Diya Or An Earthen Lamp

The earthen lamps which are used to remove darkness since Vedic time. During Lakshmi Puja she is welcomed by lighting as many as possible earthen lamps.

(Instead of earthen lamp/diya, you can also use Copper lamp)

PUJAS AND FESTIVAL CELEBRATION DEDICATED TO MAA LAKSHMI (MAHALAKSHMI)

Varalakshmi Vrata (Varamahalakshmi Puja)

The festival of *Varalakshmi Vratha* falls in the month of July or August (Shravana or Avani month- fifth month of the Hindu calendar) Shukla Paksha (Waxing Moon period)) on Last Friday. *Varalakshmi* is a goddess who grants boons ("Vara") to her devotees who keep faith on her. It is believed that worshipping the Goddess Lakshmi on this day is equivalent to worshipping Ashtalakshmi – the eight goddesses of Wealth, Earth, Wisdom, Love, Fame, Peace, Contentment, and Strength. Varalakshmi Puja is performed mostly by married women for the well-being of husband and the other family members.

Diwali Lakshmi Puja (Deepavali Lakshmi Puja)

Diwali (Deepavali) the "Festival of Lights" that is celebrated in the Hindu month of Kartika, by millions of Hindus and Jains across the world. Lakshmi Puja or Diwali Puja will be performed on Diwali day-evening, the new moon day (Ashwin Krishna Paksha Amavasya) . According puranas and vedas, Goddess Lakshmi came from the milky ocean on the day of "Dhantrayodashi" and chose Lord Vishnu as her husband on the day of Diwali.

In the traditional Hindu businesses, Diwali is considered to be the last day of the financial year. Therefore, 'Chopda Puja' is performed on this day on the new account books. Chopda Puja is also termed as 'Muhurat Puja'. During Chopda Puja new account books are inaugurated in the presence of Lakshmi and Ganesh to seek their blessing for the next financial year.

Navrathiri (Sharadiya Navratri)

Every Hindu festival has a spiritual message. This nine-day festival celebrates the triumph of good over evil.During these nine nights, the Mother Goddess is worshipped in her variously manifested forms as Durga, Lakshmi, and Saraswati. Navaratri (Sharadiya Navratri) falls on the first nine days of the Ashwin Shukla Paksha. 'Ashwin' is seventh month of theHindu calendar. Shukla paksha is the period between the New Moon 'Amavasya' to the Full Moon 'Poornima'.

Fourth, fifth and Sixth days of Navratri are committed to Goddess Maa Lakshmi, the Goddess of wealth and prosperity.

Akshaya Tritiya

Akshaya tritiya puja is mainly dedicated to goddess Maha Lakshmi and worshipping her during the day is considered very auspicious occasion by Hindus and people often buy gold on this day in the hope that it will bring good luck. Akshaya Tritiya is celebrated on the third day of the Shukla Paksha (waxing phase of the moon) during Vaisakha month as per the Hindu calendar (April or May).

Gaja Lakshmi Puja / Kojagari Lakshmi Puja

This worship is specially prevalent in East India (West Bengal, Odissha, Assam) .On this day unmarried women keep fast with the popular belief of getting their suitable groom. Gajalakshmi Puja or Kojagari Lakshmi Puja or Kumar Poornima Puja falls on Ashwin Poornima (September–October). This is a harvest festival of Prosperity, Good Luck and Abundance marking the end of monsoon season. On Kojagaari Poornima night, Goddess Lakshmi is thanked and worshiped for the harvests.

(Kojagari is a Bengaliword -meaning 'who is awake')

Auspicious Days To Please Goddess Lakshmi

Regular Lakshmi Puja blesses you wealthy and financially successful (Resolves all financial issues).

Goddess Lakshmi is worshipped on Daily or New moon day or Full Moon Day or Thursday or Friday.

(Note: Please check and verify exact dates of festival celebrations/vratha dates in Hindu calendars or Panchang)

***

POWERFUL SACRED MANTRAS FOR GODDESS LAKSHMI (PUJA)

"Let Goddess MahaLakshmi bless you with all eight forces on this Puja : Shri (Wealth), Bhu (Earth), Saraswati (learning), Priti (love), Kirti (Fame), Shanti (Peace), Tushti (Pleasure) and Pushti (Strength"

INVOCATION TO LORD GANESH

Vakra-Tunndda Maha-Kaaya Suurya-Kotti Samaprabha |
Nirvighnam Kuru Me Deva Sarva-Kaaryessu Sarvadaa ||

वक्रतुण्ड महाकाय सूर्यकोटि समप्रभ ।
निर्विघ्नं कुरु मे देव सर्वकार्येषु सर्वदा ॥

Salutations to Sri Ganesha : O Lord, Who has a Curved Trunk, Who has a Large Body, Whose aura is like light of crores of sun, Please make my entire work obstacle free, forever.

Chanting of this mantra helps to achieve wealth, wisdom, good luck, prosperity and success in all the endeavors.

SHANTHI MANTRA

Om Saha Naav (au) Avatu |
Saha Nau Bhunaktu |
Saha Viiryam Karavaavahai |
Tejasvi Naav[au]Adhii tamAstu Maa Vidvissaavahai |
Om Shaantih: Shaantih: Shaantih: ||

ॐ सह नाववतु ।
सह नौ भुनक्तु ।
सह वीर्यं करवावहै ।
तेजस्वि नावधीतमस्तु मा विद्विषावहै ।
ॐ शान्तिः शान्तिः शान्तिः ॥

This Shanti mantra, prayer for peace found in the krishna Yajurveda Taittiriya Upanishad (2.2.2).This mantra purifies the body and relieves it from the sufferings, diseases and discomforts.

Om, May He protect us both together; may He nourish us both togethe.Together may we perform . May what has been Studied by us be vigorous and effective; .Om! Let there be peace in me! May peace be unto us, and may peace be unto all living beings.

ASANA PUJA

Om Prthvi Tvayaa Dhrtaa Lokaa
Devi Tvam Vissnnunaa Dhrtaa |
Tvam Ca Dhaaraya Maam Devi
Pavitram Kuru Cha-[A]asanam ||

ॐ पृथ्वि त्वया धृता लोका
देवि त्वं विष्णुना धृता ।
त्वं च धारय मां देवि
पवित्रं कुरु चासनम् ॥

Performing the Asana puja (body Posture) while sitting on it brings knowledge, peace, wealth and Accomplishment. Woolen/Cloth/Wood puja asans are ideal for comfortable seating during puja.

Om, O Prithivi Devi /Bhoomi Devi, You are borne the entire world Please hold me O Devi, and make this seat of the worshipper Pure.

DEEPA PUJA

Shubham Karothi Kalyaannam-Aarogyam Dhana-Sampadaa | Shatru-Buddhi-Vinaashaaya Diipa-Jyotir-Namostute ||

शुभं करोति कल्याणमारोग्यं धनसंपदा ।
शत्रुबुद्धिविनाशाय दीपज्योतिर्नमोऽस्तुते ॥

Salutations to the Light of the Lamp, Which Brings Auspiciousness, Health and Prosperity; Which Destroys Inimical Feelings

GAYATRI MANTRA FOR PRANAYAMA

This 'Yajur Veda: Taittiriya Aranyaka 'strengthens our mind with concentration and gives immense peace to us.

Om Bhuuh : Om Bhuvah: Om Svah:
Om Mahah :Om Janah : Om Tapah: Om Satyam
Om Tat-Savitur Varennyam Bhargo Devasya Dhiimahi
Dhiyo Yo Nah Pracodayaat |
Om Aapo Jyotii Rasoa Amrtam
Brahma Bhuur Bhuvah: SvarOm ||

(Touch the ears three times and saying Om, Om, Om)

ॐ भूः ॐ भुवः ॐ स्वः
ॐ महः ॐ जनः ॐ तपः ॐ सत्यम्
ॐ तत्सवितुर्वरेण्यं भर्गो देवस्य धीमहि
धियो यो नः प्रचोदयात् ।
ॐ आपो ज्योती रसोऽमृतं ब्रह्म भूर्भुवः स्वरोम् ॥

Om,I meditate on the Consciousness of the Physical Plane, Om, I meditate on the intercede Space, Om, I meditate on the Heaven, Consciousness of the beginning of the Divine Mind.(the meditation goes to subtler levels)

SANKALPA MANTRA

The procedure of making a decision to perform the pooja for the welfare of all concerned.

For Saivas

Mamo partha samastha duritha kshaya dwara ,

Sri Parameshwara preethyartham

Sri Mahalakshmi prasada sidhyartham

Asmaham Sakudumbanam

shemasya, dhairyasya, dhairya, vijaya, ayur, arogya, ishwarya, abhiv-rithyartham, Kalyana Prapyartham, Sakala vasikaranartham

Mahaganaptim pujam karishye

For Vaishnavas

Mamo partha samastha duritha kshaya dwara ,

Sri Narayana Preethyartham

Sri Mahalakshmi prasada sidhyartham

Asmaham Sakudumbanam

shemasya, dhairyasya, dhairya, vijaya, ayur, arogya, ishwarya, abhiv-

rithyartham, Kalyana Prapyartham, Sakala vasikaranartham

Mahaganaptim pujam karishye

Om For removing all problems and pains in life.For making Lord happy. For blessings of Goddess Parvathi. For getting my above wishes fulfilled.

KALASH(A) PUJA

Kalashasya mukhe Vishnu: kanTe rudrassamaasrita:|
Mule tatra sthitho brahma madhye matrugana: smruta: ||
kukshou thu saagara: sarve sapthadveepa vasundhara: |
Rigvedoatha yajurveda: saama vedo atharvavana: ||
angaischa sahita ssarve kalashaambu samaasrita: |

कलशस्य मुखे विष्णु: कण्ठे रुद्र: समाश्रित:|
मूले तस्य स्थितो ब्रह्मा मध्ये मातृगणा: स्थिता ||
कुक्षौ तु सागर: सर्वे सप्तद्वीपा वसुन्धरा |
ग्वेंदो यजुर्वेद: सामवेदो अथर्वण: ||
अङ्गैश्च सहितं सर्वे कलशाम्बु समाश्रिता: |

Invite all the holy rivers like Ganga,yamuna, saraswati,narmada, godavari, sindhu,kaveri into this water pot . Invite all the gods ie Brahma, Vishnu, Shiva, Ganesh. (May come to me to bestow Peace and remove the Evil Influences)

Kalash(a) is traditionally a copper pot. Fill it up with water and put two or three leaves of tulsi leaves or flower petals as well . Take few more couple of flower petals (or Tulsi leaves) dip it in the pot water and sprinkle it around the area you are seated . Then sprinkle the few drops of water if,other people seated around you .

GHANTA PUJA

**Aagama Artham Tu Devaanaam Gamana Artham Tu Rakssasaam |
Ghannttaa Ravam Karomya(ia)adau Devataa Ahvaana Laan chanam ||**

आगमार्थं तु देवानां गमनार्थं तु रक्षसाम् ।
घण्टारवं करोम्यादौ देवताह्वान लाञ्छनम् ॥

For the purpose of inviting the Divine Forces and removing Evil Forces, I make the (Ghanta) Bell Sound.

MAHALAKSHMI MANTRA

Om Sarvabaadhaa Vinirmukto,
Dhan Dhaanyah: Sutaanvitah: |
Manushyo Matprasaaden Bhavishyati
Na Sanshayah : Om ||

ॐ सर्वाबाधा विनिर्मुक्तो, धन धान्यः सुतान्वितः।
मनुष्यो मत्प्रसादेन भविष्यति न संशयः ॐ ।।

O Goddess Mahalakshmi, eradicate all evil forces and bestow upon all a prosperous and Wealth

(Note: You can chant this mantra 3 or 9 or 18 times to get more benefit)

LAKSHMI BEEJ(AH) MANTRA

|| Om Shring Shriye(a) Namah ||

।।ॐ श्रीं श्रियें नमः ।।

This Beej (ah) Mantra is considered as origin of all powers of Goddess Lakshmi. The Mantra of Goddess Lakshmi is only Shring(श्रीं), which is combined with other words to form various Mantras.

(Note: You can chant this mantra 3 or 9 or 18 times to get more benefit)

LAKSHMI GAYATRI MANTRA

Om Shree Mahalakshmyai Cha Vidmahe
Vishnu Patnyai Cha Dheemahi
Tanno Lakshmi Prachodayat Om ||

ॐ श्री महालक्ष्म्यै च विद्महे विष्णु पत्न्यै च धीमहि
तन्नो लक्ष्मी प्रचोदयात् ॐ॥

Om, Let me meditate on the greatest goddess, Who is the wife of Lord Vishnu, provide me higher intellect, And let Goddess Lakshmi make brighter my mind.

(Note: You can chant this mantra 3 or 9 or 18 times to get prosperity and success.)

FIVE POWERFUL MANTRAS OF MAA LAKSHMI THAT BRINGS PROGRESS IN YOUR LIFE

Mantra For Business Success

Om ain shreen mahaalakshmyai kamal dhaarinyai garood vaahinyai shreen ain namah:

ॐ ऐं श्रीं महालक्ष्म्यै कमल धारिण्यै गरुड़ वाहिन्यै श्रीं ऐं नमः

Mantra For Career/Job Success

Om Hring Shring Kreeng Shring Kreeng Kling Shring Mahaalakshmi Mam Grihe Dhanam Pooray Pooray Chintaayai Dooray Dooray Swaha |

ॐ ह्री श्रीं क्रीं श्रीं क्रीं क्लीं श्रीं महालक्ष्मी मम गृहे धनं पूरय पूरय चिंतायै दूरय दूरय स्वाहा ।

Mantra For Mantra For Wealth And

Abundance.

Om Shreem Maha Lakshmiyei Namah:

ॐ श्रीं महालक्ष्म्यै नमः

Mantra For Good Fortune

om shreen hreen kleen:

ॐ श्रीं ह्रीं क्लीं:

Mantra For Happiness

Om Shreen Shree-aee Namaha

ॐ श्रीं श्रीय नम:

(Note: You can chant these mantras 3 or 9 or 18 times to get more benefit)

SRI MAHALAKSHMI ASHTAKAM

Shri Mahalakshmi Ashtakam is taken from 'Padma Purana 'and this prayer was chanted by Lord Indra. This prayer is very ancient and has been chanted by generations for solving all their problems.

Namastestu Mahaa-Maaye Shrii-Piitthe Sura-Puujite |
Shangkha-Cakra-Gadaa-Haste Mahaalakssmi Namostute ||1||

नमस्तेऽस्तु महामाये श्रीपीठे सुरपूजिते ।
शङ्खचक्रगदाहस्ते महालक्ष्मि नमोऽस्तुते ॥१॥

Namaste Garudda-Aaruuddhe Kola-Aasura-Bhayamkari |
Sarva-Paapa-Hare Devi Mahaalakssmi Namostute ||2||

नमस्ते गरूडारूढे कोलासुरभयंकरि ।
सर्वपापहरे देवि महालक्ष्मि नमोऽस्तुते ॥२॥

Sarvajnye Sarva-Varade Sarva-Dusstta-Bhayamkari |
Sarva-Duhkha-Hare Devi Mahaalakssmi Namostute ||3||

सर्वज्ञे सर्ववरदे सर्वदुष्टभयंकरि ।
सर्वदुःखहरे देवि महालक्ष्मि नमोऽस्तुते ॥३॥

Siddhi-Buddhi-Prade Devi Bhukti-Mukti-Pradaayini |
Mantra-Muurte Sadaa Devi
Mahaalakssmi Namostute ||4||

सिद्धिबुद्धिप्रदे देवि भुक्तिमुक्तिप्रदायिनि ।
मन्त्रमूर्ते सदा देवि महालक्ष्मि नमोऽस्तुते ॥४॥

Aad-Anta-Rahite Devi Aadya-Shakti-Maheshvari |
Yogaje Yoga-Sambhuute
Mahaalakssmi Namostute ||5||

आद्यन्तरहिते देवि आद्यशक्तिमहेश्वरि ।
योगजे योगसम्भूते महालक्ष्मि नमोऽस्तुते ॥५॥

Sthuula-Suukssma-Mahaaroudre Mahaa-Shakti-Mahodare |
Mahaa-Paapa-Hare Devi
Mahaalakssmi Namostute ||6||

स्थूलसूक्ष्ममहारौद्रे महाशक्तिमहोदरे ।
महापापहरे देवि महालक्ष्मि नमोऽस्तुते ॥६॥

Padma-Aasana-Sthite Devi Para-Brahma-Svaruupinni |
Parameshi Jagan-Maatar-
Mahaalakssmi Namostute ||7||

पद्मासनस्थिते देवि परब्रह्मस्वरूपिणि ।
परमेशि जगन्मातर्महालक्ष्मि नमोऽस्तुते ॥७॥

Shveta-Ambara-Dhare Devi Naana-Alangkaara-Bhuussite |
Jagatsthite Jagan-Maatar-
Mahaalakssmi Namostute ||8||

श्वेताम्बरधरे देवि नानालङ्कारभूषिते ।
जगत्स्थिते जगन्मातर्महालक्ष्मि नमोऽस्तुते ॥८॥

Mahaalakssmyassttakam Stotram Yah: Patthedbhaktimaannarah: | Sarvasiddhimavaapnoti Raajyam Praapnoti Sarvadaa ||9||

महालक्ष्म्यष्टकं स्तोत्रं यः पठेद्भक्तिमान्नरः ।
सर्वसिद्धिमवाप्नोति राज्यं प्राप्नोति सर्वदा ॥९॥

Ekakaale Patthennityam Mahaapaapavinaashanam | Dvikaalam Yah Patthennityam Dhanadhaanyasamanvitah: ||10||

एककाले पठेन्नित्यं महापापविनाशनम् ।
द्विकालं यः पठेन्नित्यं धनधान्यसमन्वितः ॥१०॥

Trikaalam Yah: Patthennityam Mahaashatruvinaashanam | Mahaalakssmirbhavennityam Prasannaa Varadaa Shubhaa ||11||

त्रिकालं यः पठेन्नित्यं महाशत्रुविनाशनम् ।
महालक्ष्मिर्भवेन्नित्यं प्रसन्ना वरदा शुभा ॥११॥

KANAKADHĀRA STOTRAM

Kanakadhara Stotram, which was composed by one of India's foremost spiritual saints, Sri Adi Shankaracharya, around 810 AD. He dedicated the Stotram to Goddess Lakshmi, set in 21 hymns. Kanak means gold, and Dhara means flow. The Kanakadhara Stotram describes the beauty, grace, wisdom, and power of the Goddess of wealth and prosperity.Chant this Kanakadhara Stotram on every Fridays, and mornings and evenings on Full Moon days. This powerful Hymns helps eliminate poverty and bring happiness also push away negative energy.

Angam hare: pulaka bhooshanamasray-anthi,
Bhringanga neva mukulabharanam thamalam |
Angikrithakhila vibhuthirapanga leela,
Mangalyadasthu mama mangala devathaya: || 1||

अङ्गं हरेः पुलकभूषणमाश्रयन्ती
भृङ्गाङ्गनेव मुकुलाभरणं तमालम् ।
अंगीकृताखिलविभूतिरपांगलीला
मांगल्यदास्तु मम मंगलदेवतायाः ॥ १ ॥

Mugdha muhurvidhadhadathi vadhane Murare:
Premathrapapranihithani gathagathani |

Mala dhrishotmadhukareeva maheth pale ya,
Sa ne sriyam dhisathu sagarasambhavaya: ||2||

मुग्धा मुहुर्विदधती वदनै मुरारेः
प्रेमत्रपाप्रणिहितानि गतागतानि ।
माला दृशोर्मधुकरीव महोत्पले या
सा मे श्रियं दिशतु सागरसंभवायाः ॥ २ ॥

Ameelithaksha madhigamya mudha Mukundam
Anandakandamanimeshamananga thanthram,
Akekara stiththa kaninika pashma nethram,
Bhoothyai bhavenmama bhjan-gasayananganaya : || 3||

आमीलिताक्षमधिगम्य मुदा मुकुन्दं
आनन्दकन्दमनिमेषमनंगतन्त्रम् ।
आकेकरस्थितकनीनिकपक्ष्मनेत्रं
भूत्यै भवेन्मम भुजंगशयांगनायाः ॥ ३ ॥

Bahwanthare madhujitha: srithakausthube ya,
Haravaleeva nari neela mayi vibhathi,
Kamapradha bhagavatho api kadaksha mala,
Kalyanamavahathu me kamalalayaya: || 4 ||

बाह्वन्तरे मधुजितः श्रितकौस्तुभे या
हारावलीव हरिनीलमयी विभाति ।
कामप्रदा भगवतोऽपि कटाक्षमाला
कल्याणमावहतु मे कमलालयायाः ॥ ४ ॥

Kalambudhaalithorasi kaida bhare:
Dharaadhare sphurathi yaa thadinganeva |
Mathu samastha jagatham mahaneeya murthy :
Badrani me dhisathu bhargava nandanaya : || 5 ||

कालाम्बुदालिललितोरसि कैटभारेः
धाराधरे स्फुरति या तटिदङ्गनेव ।
मातुस्समस्तजगतां महनीयमूर्तिः
भद्राणि मे दिशतु भार्गवनन्दनायाः ॥ ५ ॥

Praptham padam pradhamatha khalu yat prabhavath,
Mangalyabhaji madhu madhini manamathena |
Mayyapadetha mathara meekshanardham,
Manthalasam cha makaralaya kanyakaya: || 6 ||

प्राप्तं पदं प्रथमतः खलु यत्प्रभावात्
माङ्गल्यभाजि मधुमाथिनि मन्मथेन ।
मयापतेत्तदिह मन्थरमीक्षणार्धं
मन्दालसं च मकरालयकन्यकायाः ॥ ६ ॥

Viswamarendra padhavee bramadhana dhaksham,

Ananda hethu radhikam madhu vishwoapi |
Eshanna sheedhathu mayi kshanameek-shanartham,
Indhivarodhara sahodhar-amidhiraya : || 7 ||

विश्वामरेन्द्रपदविभ्रमदानदक्षं
आनन्दहेतुरधिकं मुरविद्विषोऽपि ।
ईषन्निषीदतु मयि क्षणमीक्षणार्धं
इन्दीवरोदरसहोदरमिन्दिरायाः ॥ ७ ॥

Ishta visishtamathayopi yaya dhayardhra,
Dhrishtya thravishta papadam sulabham labhanthe |
Hrishtim prahrushta kamlodhara deepthirishtam,
Pushtim krishishta mama pushkravishtaraya: || 8 ||

इष्टा विशिष्टमतयोऽपि यया दयार्द्र-
दृष्ट्या त्रिविष्टपपदं सुलभं लभन्ते ।
दृष्टिः प्रहृष्टकमलोदरदीप्तिरिष्टां
पुष्टिं कृषीष्ट मम पुष्करविष्टरायाः ॥ ८ ॥

Dhadyaddhayanupavanopi dravinambhudaraam,
Asminna kinchina vihanga sisou vishanne |
Dhushkaramagarmmapaneeya chiraya dhooram,
Narayana pranayinee

nayanambhuvaha: || 9 ||

दद्याद्दयानुपवनो द्रविणाम्बुधारां
अस्मिन्नकिञ्चनविहंगशिशौ विषण्णे ।
दुष्कर्मघर्ममपनीय चिराय दूरं
नारायणप्रणयिनीनयनाम्बुवाहः ॥ ९ ॥

Gheerdhevathethi garuda dwaja sundarithi,
Sakambhareethi sasi shekara vallebhethi |
Srishti sthithi pralaya kelishu samsthitha ya,
Thasyai namas thribhvanai ka guros tharunyai: || 10 ||

गीर्देवतेति गरुडध्वजसुन्दरीति
शाकंभरीति शशिशेखरवल्लभेति ।
सृष्टिस्थितिप्रलयकेलिषु संस्थितायै
तस्यै नमस्त्रिभुवनैकगुरोस्तरुण्यै ॥ १० ॥

Sruthyai namosthu shubha karma phala prasoothyai,
Rathyai namosthu ramaneeya gunarnavayai |
Shakthyai namosthu satha pathra nikethanayai,
Pushtayi namosthu purushotthama vallabhayai: || 11 ||

श्रुत्यै नमोऽस्तु शुभकर्मफलप्रसूत्यै
रत्यै नमोऽस्तु रमणीयगुणार्णवायै ।
शक्त्यै नमोऽस्तु शतपत्रनिकेतनायै
पुष्ट्यै नमोऽस्तु पुरुषोत्तमवल्लभायै ॥ ११ ॥

Namosthu naleekha nibhananai,
Namosthu dhugdhogdhadhi janma bhoomayai |
Namosthu somamrutha sodharayai,
Namosthu narayana vallabhayai: || 12 ||

नमोऽस्तु नालीकनिभाननायै
नमोऽस्तु दुग्धोदधिजन्मभूम्यै ।
नमोऽस्तु सोमामृतसोदरायै
नमोऽस्तु नारायणवल्लभायै ॥ १२ ॥

Namosthu hemambhuja peetikayai,
Namosthu bhoo mandala nayikayai |
Namosthu devathi dhaya prayai,
Namosthu Sarngayudha vallabhayai: || 13 ||

नमोऽस्तु हेमाम्बुजपीठिकायै
नमोऽस्तु भूमण्डलनायिकायै ।
नमोऽस्तु देवादिदयापरायै
नमोऽस्तु शाङ्गार्युधवल्लभायै ॥ १३ ॥

Namosthu devyai bhrugu nandanayai,
Namosthu vishnorurasi sthithayai |
Namosthu lakshmyai kamalalayai,
Namosthu dhamodhra vallabhayai: || 14 ||

नमोऽस्तु देव्यै भृगुनन्दनायै
नमोऽस्तु विष्णोरुरसि स्थितायै ।
नमोऽस्तु लक्ष्म्यै कमलालयायै
नमोऽस्तु दामोदरवल्लभायै ॥ १४ ॥

Namosthu Kanthyai kamalekshanayai,
Namosthu bhoothyai bhuvanaprasoothyai

|

Namosthu devadhibhir archithayai,
Namosthu nandhathmaja
vallabhayai: || 15 ||

नमोऽस्तु कान्त्यै कमलेक्षणायै
नमोऽस्तु भूत्यै भुवनप्रसूत्यै ।
नमोऽस्तु देवादिभिरर्चितायै
नमोऽस्तु नन्दात्मजवल्लभायै ॥ १५ ॥

Sampath karaani sakalendriya nandanani,
Samrajya dhana vibhavani saroruhakshi |
Twad vandanani dhuritha harano-
dhythani,
Mamev matharanisam kalayanthu
manye: || 16 ||

सम्पत्कराणि सकलेन्द्रियनन्दनानि
साम्राज्यदानविभवानि सरोरुहाक्षि ।
त्वद्वन्दनानि दुरिताहरणोद्यतानि
मामेव मातरनिशं कलयन्तु मान्ये ॥ १६ ॥

Yath Kadaksha samupasana vidhi :
Sevakasya sakalartha sapadha: |
Santhanodhi vachananga manasai :
Twaam murari hridayeswareem
bhaje: || 17 ||

यत्कटाक्षसमुपासनाविधिः
सेवकस्यसकलार्थसंपदः ।
सन्तनोतिवचनाङ्गमानसैः
त्वां मुरारि हृदयेश्वरीं भजे ॥ १७ ॥

Sarasija nilaye saroja hasthe,

Dhavalathamamsuka gandha maya shobhe |
Bhagavathi hari vallabhe manogne,
Tribhuvana bhoothikari praseeda mahye : || 18 ||

सरसिजनिलये सरोजहस्ते
धवलतरांशुकगन्धमाल्यशोभे ।
भगवति हरिवल्लभे मनोज्ञे
त्रिभुवनभूतिकरि प्रसीद मह्यम् ॥ १८ ॥

Dhiggasthibhi kanaka kumbha mukha vasrushta,
Sarvahini vimala charu jalaapluthangim |
Prathar namami jagathaam janani masesha-
Lokadhinatha grahini mamrithabhi puthreem: || 19 ||

दिग्घस्तिभिः कनककुम्भमुखावसृष्ट-
स्वर्वाहिनीविमलचारुजलाप्लुताङ्गीम् ।
प्रातर्नमामि जगतां जननीमशेष-
लोकाधिनाथगृहिणीममृताब्धिपुत्रीम् ॥ १९ ॥

Kamale Kamalaksha vallabhe twam,
Karuna poora tharingithaira pangai :|
Avalokaya mamakinchananam,
Prathamam pathamakrithrimam dhyaya : || 20 ||

कमले कमलाक्षवल्लभे त्वं
करुणापूरतरङ्गितैरपाङ्गैः ।
अवलोकय मामकिञ्चनानां

प्रथमं पात्रमकृत्रिमं दयायाः ॥ २० ॥

Sthuvanthi ye sthuthibhirameeranwa-ham,
Thrayeemayim thribhuvanamatharam ramam |
Gunadhika guruthara bhagya bhagina :
Bhavanthi the bhuvi budha bhavithasayo: || 21 ||

स्तुवन्ति ये स्तुतिभिरमीभिरन्वहं
त्रयीमयीं त्रिभुवनमातरं रमाम् ।
गुणाधिका गुरुतरभाग्यभागिनः
भवन्ति ते भुवि बुधभाविताशयाः ॥ २१ ॥

ŚRĪ SŪKTA(M)

Sri Suktham is an invocation to Goddess Lakshmi from appendices to the Rigveda. This collection of mantras can bring immense material benefits and negate financial hardships. This ritual can confer health, wealth, peace and prosperity and bring about abundance in your life.

Harih Om

हरिः ॐ

Hirannya-Varnnaam Harinniim
Suvarnna-Rajata-Srajaam |
Candraam Hirannmayiim Lakssmiim
Jaatavedo Ma Aavaha ||1||

हिरण्यवर्णां हरिणीं सुवर्णरजतस्रजाम् ।
चन्द्रां हिरण्मयीं लक्ष्मीं जातवेदो म आवह ॥१॥

Taam Ma Aavaha Jaatavedo Lakssmiim-
Anapagaaminiim |
Yasyaam Hirannyam Vindeyam Gaam-
Ashvam Purussaan-Aham ||2||

तां म आवह जातवेदो लक्ष्मीमनपगामिनीम् ।
यस्यां हिरण्यं विन्देयं गामश्वं पुरुषानहम् ॥२॥

Ashva-Puurvaam Ratha-Madhyaam
Hastinaada-Prabodhiniim |
Shriyam Deviim-Upahvaye
Shriirmaa Devii Jussataam ||3||

अश्वपूर्वां रथमध्यां हस्तिनादप्रबोधिनीम् ।
श्रियं देवीमुपह्वये श्रीर्मा देवी जुषताम् ॥३॥

**Kaam So-Smitaam Hirannya-
Praakaaraam-Aardraam Jvalantiim
Trptaam Tarpayantiim |
Padme Sthitaam Padma-Varnnaam
Taam-Iho[a-u]pahvaye Shriyam ||4||**

कां सोस्मितां हिरण्यप्राकारामार्द्रां ज्वलन्तीं तृप्तां तर्पयन्तीम् ।
पद्मे स्थितां पद्मवर्णां तामिहोपह्वये श्रियम् ॥४॥

**Candraam Prabhaasaam Yashasaa
Jvalantiim Shriyam Loke Deva-
Jussttaam-Udaaraam |
Taam Padminiim-Iim Sharannam-
Aham Prapadye-[A]lakssmiir-Me
Nashyataam Tvaam Vrnne ||5||**

चन्द्रां प्रभासां यशसा ज्वलन्तीं श्रियं लोके देवजुष्टामुदाराम् ।
तां पद्मिनीमीं शरणमहं प्रपद्येऽलक्ष्मीर्मे नश्यतां त्वां वृणे ॥५॥

**Aaditya-Varnne Tapaso[a-A]dhi-Jaato
Vanaspatis-Tava Vrksso[ah-A]tha Bilvah |
Tasya Phalaani Tapasaa-Nudantu Maaya-
Antaraayaashca Baahyaa Alakssmiih ||6||**

आदित्यवर्णे तपसोऽधिजातो वनस्पतिस्तव वृक्षोऽथ बिल्वः ।
तस्य फलानि तपसानुदन्तु मायान्तरायाश्च बाह्या अलक्ष्मीः ॥६॥

**Upaitu Maam Deva-Sakhah Kiirtish-
Ca Manninaa Saha |**

Praadurbhuuto[ah-A]smi Raassttre-[A]smin Kiirtim-Rddhim Dadaatu Me ||7||

उपैतु मां देवसखः कीर्तिश्च मणिना सह ।
प्रादुर्भूतोऽस्मि राष्ट्रेऽस्मिन् कीर्तिमृद्धिं ददातु मे ॥७॥

**Kssut-Pipaasaa-Malaam Jyesstthaam-Alakssmiim Naashayaamy-Aham |
Abhuutim-Asamrddhim Ca Sarvaam Nirnnuda Me Grhaat ||8||**

क्षुत्पिपासामलां ज्येष्ठामलक्ष्मीं नाशयाम्यहम् ।
अभूतिमसमृद्धिं च सर्वां निर्णुद मे गृहात् ॥८॥

**Gandha-Dvaaraam Duraadharssaam Nitya-Pussttaam Kariissinniim |
Iishvariing Sarva-Bhuutaanaam Taam-Iho[a-u]pahvaye Shriyam ||9||**

गन्धद्वारां दुराधर्षां नित्यपुष्टां करीषिणीम् ।
ईश्वरींग् सर्वभूतानां तामिहोपह्वये श्रियम् ॥९॥

**Manasah Kaamam-Aakuutim Vaacah Satyam-Ashiimahi |
Pashuunaam Ruupam-Annasya Mayi Shriih Shrayataam Yashah ||10||**

मनसः काममाकूतिं वाचः सत्यमशीमहि ।
पशूनां रूपमन्नस्य मयि श्रीः श्रयतां यशः ॥१०॥

**Kardamena Prajaa-Bhuutaa Mayi Sambhava Kardama |
Shriyam Vaasaya Me Kule Maataram**

Padma-Maaliniim ||11||

कर्दमेन प्रजाभूता मयि सम्भव कर्दम ।
श्रियं वासय मे कुले मातरं पद्ममालिनीम् ॥११॥

Aapah Srjantu Snigdhaani Cikliita Vasa Me Grhe | Ni Ca Deviim Maataram Shriyam Vaasaya Me Kule ||12||

आपः सृजन्तु स्निग्धानि चिक्लीत वस मे गृहे ।
नि च देवीं मातरं श्रियं वासय मे कुले ॥१२॥

Aardraam Pusskarinniim Pussttim Pinggalaam Padma-Maaliniim | Candraam Hirannmayiim Lakssmiim Jaatavedo Ma Aavaha ||13||

आर्द्रां पुष्करिणीं पुष्टिं पिङ्गलां पद्ममालिनीम् ।
चन्द्रां हिरण्मयीं लक्ष्मीं जातवेदो म आवह ॥१३॥

Aardraam Yah Karinniim Yassttim Suvarnnaam Hema-Maaliniim | Suuryaam Hirannmayiim Lakssmiim Jaatavedo Ma Aavaha ||14||

आर्द्रां यः करिणीं यष्टिं सुवर्णां हेममालिनीम् ।
सूर्यां हिरण्मयीं लक्ष्मीं जातवेदो म आवह ॥१४॥

Taam Ma Aavaha Jaatavedo Lakssmiim-Anapagaaminiim | Yasyaam Hirannyam Prabhuutam Gaavo Daasyo-[A]shvaan Vindeyam

Puurussaan-Aham ||15||

तां म आवह जातवेदो लक्ष्मीमनपगामिनीम् ।
यस्यां हिरण्यं प्रभूतं गावो दास्योऽश्वान् विन्देयं पूरुषानहम् ॥१५॥

**Yah Shucih Prayato Bhuutvaa Juhu-
Yaad-Aajyam-Anvaham |
Suuktam Pan.cadasharcam Ca
Shriikaamah Satatam Japet ||16||**

यः शुचिः प्रयतो भूत्वा जुहुयादाज्यमन्वहम् ।
सूक्तं पञ्चदशर्चं च श्रीकामः सततं जपेत् ॥१६॥

**Padma-[A]anane Padma Uuru Padma-
Akssii Padmaa-Sambhave |
Tvam Maam Bhajasva Padma-Akssii Yena
Saukhyam Labhaamy[i]-Aham ||17|**

पद्मानने पद्म ऊरु पद्माक्षी पद्मासम्भवे ।
त्वं मां भजस्व पद्माक्षी येन सौख्यं लभाम्यहम् ॥१७॥

**Ashva-Daayi Go-Daayi Dhana-
Daayi Mahaa-Dhane |
Dhanam Me Jussataam Devi Sarva-
Kaamaamsh-Ca Dehi Me ||18||**

अश्वदायि गोदायि धनदायि महाधने ।
धनं मे जुषतां देवि सर्वकामांश्च देहि मे ॥१८॥

**Putra-Pautra Dhanam Dhaanyam
Hasty-Ashva-[A]adi-Gave Ratham |
Prajaanaam Bhavasi Maataa
Aayussmantam Karotu Maam ||19||**

पुत्रपौत्र धनं धान्यं हस्त्यश्वादिगवे रथम् ।
प्रजानां भवसि माता आयुष्मन्तं करोतु माम् ॥१९॥

**Dhanam-Agnir-Dhanam Vaayur-
Dhanam Suuryo Dhanam Vasuh |
Dhanam-Indro Brhaspatir-Varunnam
Dhanam-Ashnute ||20||**

धनमग्निर्धनं वायुर्धनं सूर्यो धनं वसुः ।
धनमिन्द्रो बृहस्पतिर्वरुणं धनमश्नुते ॥२०॥

**Vainateya Somam Piba Somam
Pibatu Vrtrahaa |
Somam Dhanasya Somino Mahyam
Dadaatu Sominah ||21||**

वैनतेय सोमं पिब सोमं पिबतु वृत्रहा ।
सोमं धनस्य सोमिनो मह्यं ददातु सोमिनः ॥२१॥

**Na Krodho Na Ca Maatsarya Na
Lobho Na-Ashubhaa Matih |
Bhavanti Krtapunnyaanaam Bhaktaanaam
Shriisuuktam Japet-Sadaa ||22||**

न क्रोधो न च मात्सर्यं न लोभो नाशुभा मतिः ।
भवन्ति कृतपुण्यानां भक्तानां श्रीसूक्तं जपेत्सदा ॥२२॥

**Varssantu Te Vibhaavari Divo
Abhrasya Vidyutah |
Rohantu Sarva-Biija-Anyava
Brahma Dvisso Jahi ||23||**

वर्षन्तु ते विभावरि दिवो अभ्रस्य विद्युतः ।

रोहन्तु सर्वबीजान्यव ब्रह्म द्विषो जहि ॥२३॥

Padma-Priye Padmini Padma-Haste Padma-[A]alaye Padma-Dalaayata-Akssi | Vishva-Priye Vissnnu Mano-[A]nukuule Tvat-Paada-Padmam Mayi Sannidhatsva ||24||

पद्मप्रिये पद्मिनि पद्महस्ते पद्मालये पद्मदलायताक्षि ।
विश्वप्रिये विष्णु मनोऽनुकूले त्वत्पादपद्मं मयि सन्निधत्स्व ॥२४॥

Yaa Saa Padma-[A]asana-Sthaa Vipula-Kattitattii Padma-Patraayata-Akssii | Gambhiiraa Varta-Naabhih Stanabhara Na-mitaa Shubhra Vastro[a-u]ttariiyaa ||25||

या सा पद्मासनस्था विपुलकटितटी पद्मपत्रायताक्षी ।
गम्भीरा वर्तनाभिः स्तनभर नमिता शुभ्र वस्त्रोत्तरीया ॥२५॥

**Lakssmiir-Divyair-Gajendrair-Manni-Ganna-Khacitais-Snaapitaa Hema-Kumbhaih |
Nityam Saa Padma-Hastaa Mama Vasatu Grhe Sarva-Maanggalya-Yuktaa ||26||**

लक्ष्मीर्दिव्यैर्गजेन्द्रैर्मणिगणखचितैस्स्नापिता हेमकुम्भैः ।
नित्यं सा पद्महस्ता मम वसतु गृहे सर्वमाङ्गल्ययुक्ता ॥२६॥

Lakssmiim Kssiira-Samudra Raaja-Tan-ayaam Shriirangga-Dhaame[a-Ii]shvariim | Daasii-Bhuuta-Samasta Deva Vanitaam Loka-i[e]ka Diipa-Amkuraam ||27||

लक्ष्मीं क्षीरसमुद्र राजतनयां श्रीरङ्गधामेश्वरीम् ।
दासीभूतसमस्त देव वनितां लोकैक दीपांकुराम् ॥२७॥

**Shriiman[t]-Manda-Kattaakssa-Labdha Vibhava Brahme(a-I)ndra-Ganggaadharaam |
Tvaam Trai-Lokya Kuttumbiniim
Sarasijaam Vande Mukunda-Priyaam ||28||**

श्रीमन्मन्दकटाक्षलब्ध विभव ब्रह्मेन्द्रगङ्गाधराम् ।
त्वां त्रैलोक्य कुटुम्बिनीं सरसिजां वन्दे मुकुन्दप्रियाम् ॥२८॥

**Siddha-Lakssmiir-Mokssa-Lakssmiir-Jaya-Lakssmiis-Sarasvatii |
Shrii-Lakssmiir-Vara-Lakssmiishca
Prasannaa Mama Sarvadaa ||29||**

सिद्धलक्ष्मीर्मोक्षलक्ष्मीर्जयलक्ष्मीस्सरस्वती ।
श्रीलक्ष्मीर्वरलक्ष्मीश्च प्रसन्ना मम सर्वदा ॥२९॥

**Vara-Angkushau Paasham-Abhiiti-Mudraam Karair-Vahantiim Kamala-[A]asana-Sthaam |
Baala-[A]arka Kotti Pratibhaam Tri-Netraam Bhaje-[A]ham-Aadyaam
Jagad-Iisvariim Tvaam ||30||**

वरांकुशौ पाशमभीतिमुद्रां करैर्वहन्तीं कमलासनस्थाम् ।
बालार्क कोटि प्रतिभां त्रिणेत्रां भजेहमाद्यां जगदीस्वरीं त्वाम् ॥३०॥

**Sarva-Manggala-Maanggalye
Shive Sarva-Artha Saadhike |
Sharannye Try-Ambake Devi**

Naaraayanni Namostu Te ||
Naaraayanni Namostu Te ||
Naaraayanni Namostu Te ||31||

सर्वमङ्गलमाङ्गल्ये शिवे सर्वार्थ साधिके ।
शरण्ये त्र्यम्बके देवि नारायणि नमोऽस्तु ते ॥
नारायणि नमोऽस्तु ते ॥ नारायणि नमोऽस्तु ते ॥३१॥

Sarasija-Nilaye Saroja-Haste Dhavalatara-Amshuka Gandha-Maalya-Shobhe |
Bhagavati Hari-Vallabhe Manojnye Tri-Bhuvana-Bhuuti-Kari Prasiida Mahyam ||32||

सरसिजनिलये सरोजहस्ते धवलतरांशुक गन्धमाल्यशोभे ।
भगवति हरिवल्लभे मनोज्ञे त्रिभुवनभूतिकरि प्रसीद मह्यम् ॥३२॥

Vissnnu-Patniim Kssamaam Deviim Maadhaviim Maadhava-Priyaam |
Vissnnoh Priya-Sakhiim Deviim Namaamy-Acyuta-Vallabhaam ||33||

विष्णुपत्नीं क्षमां देवीं माधवीं माधवप्रियाम् ।
विष्णोः प्रियसखीं देवीं नमाम्यच्युतवल्लभाम् ॥३३॥

Mahaalakssmii Ca Vidmahe Vissnnu-Patnii Ca Dhiimahi |
Tan[t]-No Lakssmiih Pracodayaat ||34||

महालक्ष्मी च विद्महे विष्णुपत्नी च धीमहि ।
तन्नो लक्ष्मीः प्रचोदयात् ॥३४॥

Shrii-Varcasyam-Aayussyam-Aarogya-

maa-Vidhaat Pavamaanam Mahiyate |
Dhanam Dhaanyam Pashum Bahu-
Putra-Laabham Shatasamvatsaram
Diirgham-Aayuh ||35||

श्रीवर्चस्यमायुष्यमारोग्यमाविधात् पवमानं महियते ।
धनं धान्यं पशुं बहुपुत्रलाभं शतसंवत्सरं दीर्घमायुः ॥३५॥

(k)runa-Roga-[A]adi-Daaridrya-
Paapa-Kssud-Apamrtyavah |
Bhaya-Shoka-Manastaapaa Nashyantu
Mama Sarvadaa ||36||

ऋणरोगादिदारिद्र्यपापक्षुदपमृत्यवः ।
भयशोकमनस्तापा नश्यन्तु मम सर्वदा ॥३६॥

Ya Evam Veda |
Om Mahaa-Devyai Ca Vidmahe
Vissnnu-Patnii Ca Dhiimahi |
Tanno Lakssmiih Pracodayaat
Om Shaantih Shaantih Shaantih ||37||

य एवं वेद ।
ॐ महादेव्यै च विद्महे विष्णुपत्नी च धीमहि ।
तन्नो लक्ष्मीः प्रचोदयात्
ॐ शान्तिः शान्तिः शान्तिः ॥३७॥

MAHALAKSHMI AŚHṬOTARA SATA NĀMĀVAḺI

Ashtottara Shatanamavali means collective hundred and eight names of God or Goddess. 108 has been considered a sacred number in Hinduism.We find many Ashtottara Shatanamavalis in Puranas as well as in epics like Mahabharata. These names are composed by Rishis, devotees, divine beings etc.

oṃ prakṛtyai namaḥ:|
ॐ प्रकृत्यै नमः|

oṃ vikṛutyai namaḥ:|
ॐ विकृत्यै नमः|

oṃ vidyāyai namaḥ:|
ॐ विद्यायै नमः|

oṃ sarvabhūtahitapradāyai namaḥ:|
ॐ सर्वभूतहितप्रदायै नमः|

oṃ śraddhāyai namaḥ:|
ॐ श्रद्धायै नमः|

oṃ vibhūtyai namaḥ:|
ॐ विभूत्यै नमः|

oṃ surabhyai namaḥ:|
ॐ सुरभ्यै नमः|

oṃ paramātmikāyai namaḥ:|

ॐ परमात्मिकायै नमः।

oṃ vāc(h)e namaḥ:|
ॐ वाचे नमः।

oṃ padmālayāyai namaḥ:|10|
ॐ पद्मालयायै नमः।10।

oṃ padmāyai namaḥ:|
ॐ पद्मायै नमः।

oṃ śucyai namaḥ:|
ॐ शुच्यै नमः।

oṃ svāhāyai namaḥ:|
ॐ स्वाहायै नमः।

oṃ svadhāyai namaḥ:|
ॐ स्वधायै नमः।

oṃ sudhāyai namaḥ:|
ॐ सुधायै नमः।

oṃ dhanyāyai namaḥ:|
ॐ धन्यायै नमः।

oṃ hiraṇmayyai namaḥ:|
ॐ हिरण्मय्यै नमः।

oṃ lakṣmyai namaḥ:|
ॐ लक्ष्म्यै नमः।

oṃ nityapuṣṭāyai namaḥ:|
ॐ नित्यपुष्टायै नमः।

oṃ vibhāvaryai namaḥ:|20|
ॐ विभावर्यै नमः।20।

oṃ adithyai namaḥ:|

ॐ अदित्यै नमः।

oṃ dithyai namaḥ:|
ॐ दित्यै नमः।

oṃ dīptāyai namaḥ:|
ॐ दीप्तायै नमः।

oṃ vasudhāyai namaḥ:|
ॐ वसुधायै नमः।

oṃ vasudhāriṇyai namaḥ:|
ॐ वसुधारिण्यै नमः।

oṃ kamalāyai namaḥ:|
ॐ कमलायै नमः।

oṃ kāntāyai namaḥ:|
ॐ कान्तायै नमः।

oṃ kāmākṣyai namaḥ:|
ॐ कामाक्ष्यै नमः।

oṃ krodhasambhavāyai namaḥ:|
ॐ क्रोधसम्भवायै नमः।

oṃ anugrahaparāyai namaḥ:|30|
ॐ अनुग्रहपरायै नमः।30।

oṃ (k)ṛddhaye namaḥ:|
ॐ ऋद्धये नमः।

oṃ anaghāyai namaḥ:|
ॐ अनघायै नमः।

oṃ harivallabhāyai namaḥ:|
ॐ हरिवल्लभायै नमः।

oṃ aśokāyai namaḥ:|
ॐ अशोकायै नमः।

oṃ amṛtāyai namaḥ:|
ॐ अमृतायै नमः|

oṃ dīptāyai namaḥ:|
ॐ दीप्तायै नमः|

oṃ lokaśoka vināśinyai namaḥ:|
ॐ लोकशोक विनाशिन्यै नमः|

oṃ dharmanilayāyai namaḥ:|
ॐ धर्मनिलयायै नमः|

oṃ karuṇāyai namaḥ:|
ॐ करुणायै नमः|

oṃ lokamātre namaḥ:|40|
ॐ लोकमात्रे नमः|40|

oṃ padmapriyāyai namaḥ:|
ॐ पद्मप्रियायै नमः|

oṃ padmahastāyai namaḥ:|
ॐ पद्महस्तायै नमः|

oṃ padmākṣyai namaḥ:|
ॐ पद्माक्ष्यै नमः|

oṃ padmasundaryai namaḥ:|
ॐ पद्मसुन्दर्यै नमः|

oṃ padmodbhavāyai namaḥ:|
ॐ पद्मोद्भवायै नमः|

oṃ padmamukhyai namaḥ:|
ॐ पद्ममुख्यै नमः|

oṃ padmanābhapriyāyai namaḥ:|
ॐ पद्मनाभप्रियायै नमः|

oṃ ramāyai namaḥ:|
ॐ रमायै नमः|

oṃ padmamālādharāyai namaḥ:|
ॐ पद्ममालाधरायै नमः|

oṃ devyai namaḥ:|50|
ॐ देव्यै नमः|50|

oṃ padminyai namaḥ:|
ॐ पद्मिन्यै नमः|

oṃ padmaganthinyai namaḥ:|
ॐ पद्मगन्थिन्यै नमः|

oṃ puṇyagandhāyai namaḥ:|
ॐ पुण्यगन्धायै नमः|

oṃ suprasannāyai namaḥ:|
ॐ सुप्रसन्नायै नमः|

oṃ prasādābhimukhyai namaḥ:|
ॐ प्रसादाभिमुख्यै नमः|

oṃ prabhāyai namaḥ:|
ॐ प्रभायै नमः|

oṃ candravadanāyai namaḥ:|
ॐ चन्द्रवदनायै नमः|

oṃ candrāyai namaḥ:|
ॐ चन्द्रायै नमः|

oṃ candrasahodaryai namaḥ:|
ॐ चन्द्रसहोदर्यै नमः|

oṃ caturbhujāyai namaḥ:|60|
ॐ चतुर्भुजायै नमः|60|

oṃ candrarūpāyai namaḥ:|
ॐ चन्द्ररूपायै नमः|

oṃ indirāyai namaḥ:|
ॐ इन्दिरायै नमः|

oṃ induśītulāyai namaḥ:|
ॐ इन्दुशीतुलायै नमः|

oṃ āhlodajananyai namaḥ:|
ॐ आह्लोदजनन्यै नमः|

oṃ puṣṭyai namaḥ:|
ॐ पुष्ट्यै नमः|

oṃ śivāyai namaḥ:|
ॐ शिवायै नमः|

oṃ śivakaryai namaḥ:|
ॐ शिवकर्यै नमः|

oṃ satyai namaḥ:|
ॐ सत्यै नमः|

oṃ vimalāyai namaḥ:|
ॐ विमलायै नमः|

oṃ viśvajananyai namaḥ |70|
ॐ विश्वजनन्यै नमः|70|

oṃ tuṣṭyai namaḥ:|
ॐ तुष्ट्यै नमः|

oṃ dāridrya nāśinyai namaḥ:|
ॐ दारिद्र्य नाशिन्यै नमः|

oṃ prītipuṣkariṇyai namaḥ:|
ॐ प्रीतिपुष्करिण्यै नमः|

oṃ śāntāyai namaḥ:|
ॐ शान्तायै नमः|

oṃ śuklamālyāmbarāyai namaḥ:|
ॐ शुक्लमाल्याम्बरायै नमः|

oṃ śriyai namaḥ:|
ॐ श्रियै नमः|

oṃ bhāskaryai namaḥ:|
ॐ भास्कर्यै नमः|

oṃ bilvanilayāyai namaḥ:|
ॐ बिल्वनिलयायै नमः|

oṃ varārohāyai namaḥ:|
ॐ वरारोहायै नमः|

oṃ yaśasvinyai namaḥ:|80|
ॐ यशस्विन्यै नमः|80|

oṃ vasundharāyai namaḥ:|
ॐ वसुन्धरायै नमः|

oṃ udārāṅgāyai namaḥ:|
ॐ उदाराङ्गायै नमः|

oṃ hariṇyai namaḥ:|
ॐ हरिण्यै नमः|

oṃ hemamālinyai namaḥ:|
ॐ हेममालिन्यै नमः|

oṃ dhanadhānya karyai namaḥ:|
ॐ धनधान्य कर्यै नमः|

oṃ siddhaye namaḥ:|
ॐ सिद्धये नमः|

oṃ straiṇa saumyāyai namaḥ:|
ॐ स्त्रैण सौम्यायै नमः।

oṃ śubhapradāyai namaḥ:|
ॐ शुभप्रदायै नमः।

oṃ nṛpaveśma gatānandāyai namaḥ:|
ॐ नृपवेश्म गतानन्दायै नमः।

oṃ varalakṣmyai namaḥ:|90|
ॐ वरलक्ष्म्यै नमः।90।

oṃ vasupradāyai namaḥ:|
ॐ वसुप्रदायै नमः।

oṃ śubhāyai namaḥ:|
ॐ शुभायै नमः।

oṃ hiraṇyaprākārāyai namaḥ:|
ॐ हिरण्यप्राकारायै नमः।

oṃ samudra tanayāyai namaḥ:|
ॐ समुद्र तनयायै नमः।

oṃ jayāyai namaḥ:|
ॐ जयायै नमः।

oṃ maṅgaḷāyai namaḥ:|
ॐ मङ्गलायै नमः।

oṃ devyai namaḥ:|
ॐ देव्यै नमः।

oṃ viṣṇu vakṣaḥsthala sthitāyai namaḥ:|
ॐ विष्णु वक्षःस्थल स्थितायै नमः।

oṃ viṣṇupatnyai namaḥ:|
ॐ विष्णुपत्न्यै नमः।

oṃ prasannākṣyai namaḥ:|100|
ॐ प्रसन्नाक्ष्यै नमः|100|

oṃ nārāyaṇa samāśritāyai namaḥ:|
ॐ नारायण समाश्रितायै नमः|

oṃ dāridrya dhvaṃsinyai namaḥ:|
ॐ दारिद्र्य ध्वंसिन्यै नमः|

oṃ sarvopadrava vāriṇyai namaḥ:|
ॐ सर्वोपद्रव वारिण्यै नमः|

oṃ navadurgāyai namaḥ:|
ॐ नवदुर्गायै नमः|

oṃ mahākāḷyai namaḥ:|
ॐ महाकाल्यै नमः|

oṃ brahma viṣṇu śivātmikāyai namaḥ:|
ॐ ब्रह्म विष्णु शिवात्मिकायै नमः|

oṃ trikāla ṅñāna sampannāyai namaḥ:|
ॐ त्रिकाल ज्ञान सम्पन्नायै नमः|

oṃ bhuvaneśvaryai namaḥ:|108|
ॐ भुवनेश्वर्यै नमः|108|

This Mahalakshmi Asthotara Sata Namavali comprises of the 108 names of Goddess Lakshmi and it is advised for everyone looking for positivity and to gain high and pure happiness.

Chanting this mantra will bring youth, beauty, happiness and money to one, which will make a great difference in life.

PRAYER

Om Sarve Bhavantu Sukhinah
Sarve Santu Nir-Aamayaah |
Sarve Bhadraanni Pashyantu
Maa Kashcid-Duhkha-Bhaag-Bhavet |
Om Shaantih Shaantih Shaantih ||

ॐ सर्वे भवन्तु सुखिनः
सर्वे सन्तु निरामयाः ।
सर्वे भद्राणि पश्यन्तु
मा कश्चिद्दुःखभाग्भवेत् ।
ॐ शान्तिः शान्तिः शान्तिः ॥

Om, May All be prosperous and happy. May all be Free from Illness.May All See what is Auspicious and spiritually uplifting. May Nobody suffer.Om Peace, Peace, Peace.

*****

ANNEXURE

POPULAR LAKSHMI TEMPLES IN INDIA

Maharashtra

Shri Ambabai (Mahalakshmi)Temple
Kolhapur, 230 KM from Pune City
URL: https://mahalaxmikolhapur.com/

Shri Mahalakshmi Temple,
Bhulabhai Desai Road, Mumbai -26
http://mahalakshmi-temple.com/

MahalaxmiTemple
Mumbai - Ahamedabad Highway
Dahanu (4 km from Charoti), Palghar

Laxminarayan Temple (Also Known As Birla Mandir) - Across India

- ✓ Near Gol Market, Mandir Marg, Connought Place, NewDelhi
- ✓ Arera Hills, Bhopal (Madhya Pradesh)
- ✓ Jawaharlal Nehru Marg,Jaipur (Rajasthan)
- ✓ Dujra Diara,Patna (Bihar)
- ✓ Brajrajnagar (Jharsuguda District, Odisha)
- ✓ Sarvodaya Nagar,Kanpur (Uttar Pradesh)
- ✓ Budhwarpet,Kurnool (Andhrapradesh)

Delhi

Lakshmi Vinayak Mandir, Chattarpur Temple, Delhi
Chhatarpur Temple is located in a down town

area in south Delhi. There are captivating idols of deities like Katyayani, Laxmi-Ganesh, Shiva-Parvati, and Hanuman.
https://www.chhattarpurmandir.org/

Karnataka

Sri Mookambika (Tri Devi)
Kollur -Udupi District (Karnataka)
https://www.kollurmookambika.org

Sri Mahalakshmi Temple
Hethenahalli,Goravanahalli, Tumkur ((Near Bengaluru,
Karnataka)
http://hethenahalliamma.com/goravanahalli-mahalakshmi-temple/

Mahalakshmi Temple
Gubbi ,Tumkur ((Near Bengaluru, Karnataka)

Lakshmi Devi Temple
Doddagaddavalli,Hassan (Near Bengaluru, Karnataka)

Mahalakshmi Temples In Bengaluru, Karnataka

- ✓ Sri Prasanna Mahalakshmi Sannidhi,Mahalakshmi Layout
- ✓ Mahalakshmi Temple,Indira Nagar,BDA Colony, 2nd stage, Domlur

- ✓ Sri Mahalakshmi Temple,Koramangala 8th Block, Adugodi
- ✓ Kempapura Mahalakshmi Temple,Hebbal
- ✓ Mahalaxmi Temple,Basaveshwar Nagar
- ✓ Sri Mahalakshmi Temple, VV Giri Colony, Seshadripuram
- ✓ lakshmi Venkateshwara Temple,Austin Town, Neelasandra
- ✓ Kollapura Mahalakshmi Temple, J. P. Nagar
- ✓ Sri Mahalakshmi Temple,Bhuvaneshwari Nagar, Banashankari
- ✓ Shree Vara Mahalakshmi Temple,Jogupalya Rd,Halsuru

Tamilnadu

Sri Lakshmi Narayani Golden Temple
Sripuram,Vellore (Tamilnadu)
https://sripuram.org/

Shri Ashtalakshmi Temple,
Besant Nagar,Chennai (Tamilnadu)
http://ashtalakshmitemple.tnhrce.in/

Abaya Hastha Swayambu Sri Lakshmi Narasimha Swamy Temple,
Agaram Village, Hosur (Tamilnadu)

Lakshmi Narayana Perumal Temple
Nachiar Kovil or Thirunarayur Nambi Temple,outskirts of Kumbakonam (Tamilnadu)

Andhrapradesh & Telungana

Shri Ashtalakshmi Temple
Outskirts Of Hyderabad (Andhrapradesh)
http://ashtalakshmitemple.co.in/

Sri Lakshmi Narasimha Swamy Temple
Dharmapuri,Jagityal,Karimnagar (Telangana)
http://www.endowments.ts.nic.in/Temple-content/dharmapuri/content.pdf

Sri Kanaka Maha Lakshmi Temple
Burujupeta,Vishakhapatnam (Andhrapradesh)
http://www.srikanakamahalakshmitemple.org/sevas.html

Madhyapradesh

Lakshmi Temple
ocated in the Western Group of Temple, Khajuraho (Madhyapradesh)

Rajasthan

Kaila Devi Temple
Kailadevi Village, Karauli (Rajasthan)
https://www.kailadevitemple.com/

Lakshmi Temples In Kerala

✓ Sree Lakshmi Varahamoorthy Temple,

Muttathara, Thiruvananthapuram

- ✓ Kadavil Sri Mahalakshmi Temple,Pallipuram
- ✓ Sree Mahalakshmi Temple,Panangad, Kochi
- ✓ Kanakadhara Mahalakshmi Temple ,Punnorkode
- ✓ Mahalakshmi Temple,Chevoor, Thrissur
- ✓ Lakshmi Temple,Melamuri, Palakkad
- ✓ Sree Lakshmi Venkatesh Temple(Kashi Math), Karattuvayal, Kanhangad
- ✓ Sree Maha Lakshmi Temple,Mananthavady

Lakshmi Temples In West Bengal

- ✓ Lakshmi Narayan Temple ,5, 1A, Paddapukur Ln, Chakraberia, Ballygunge, Kolkata
- ✓ Lakshmi ji mandir, 69, Dr Sudhir Bose Rd, Ekbalpur, Khidirpur, Kolkata
- ✓ Lakshmi Mandir, A/98, Lakshminagar, South Dumdum
- ✓ Lakshmi Temple, Anantarampur
- ✓ Lakshmi Narayan Temple, Itadangra Rd, Keshiara
- ✓ Laxmi Temple, Jukibheri
- ✓ Banokpata Laxmi Temple, Khanchi
- ✓ Lakshmi Narayan Temple,12, Natun Nagar, Taratala, Maheshtala
- ✓ Visha Lakshmi Mandir,Nasibpur, Purusattampur
- ✓ Maa Laxmi Temple,Sutaboi
- ✓ Maa Laxmi Temple,Ghoshgram
- ✓ Lakshmi Janardan Temple,Mangalpur

Lakshmi Temples In Oddisha

- ✓ Lakshmi Narayan Temple, Aiginia Over Bridge, Near NH 5, Aiginia, Bhubaneswar
- ✓ Mahalakshmi Temple, Near Lewis Road, Sisupalgarh, Bhubaneswar
- ✓ Laxmi Temple,Rental Colony Rd, Rental Colony, IRC Village, Nayapalli, Bhubaneswar
- ✓ Laxmi Narayan Temple,Adivasi Ground Rd, Unit 1, Bapuji Nagar, Bhubaneswar
- ✓ Laxmi Narayan Temple, NILAKANTH, Nilakantha Nagar, Nayapalli, Bhubaneswar
- ✓ Maa Laxmi Temple,New Railway Colony, Puri
- ✓ Lakshmi Narayan Temple, IMFA factory of Therubali, Gujalpadu, Rayagada district
- ✓ Maa Laxmi Temple,Sainik School Rd, Near Jagannath Temple, Mancheswar Industrial Estate, Mancheswar, Bhubaneswar
- ✓ Laxmi Mandir,341, N1, Block N1, IRC Village, Nayapalli, Bhubaneswar
- ✓ Sri Lakshmi Varaha Jew Temple, Demal,Kendrapara (District)
- ✓ Sri Lakshmi Narasimha Swamy Temple (SUKUNDA MATH), Chandinia Hill, Sukunda
- ✓ Maa Shanti Laxmi Temple,Barpali
- ✓ Lakshmi Narayan Temple,Unnamed Road, Badakhetabijayakrushnasaranpur

Lakshmi Temples In North East

- ✓ Lakshmi Temple,Japorigog, Guwahati, Assam
- ✓ Sawkuchi Lakshmi Mandir,Hockey Stadium Rd, Sawkuchi, Guwahati, Assam
- ✓ Lakshmi Mandir,GS Rd, Six Mile, Guwahati, Assam
- ✓ Lakshmi Mandir, Ambikagiri Nagar Path, RBI Colony, Guwahati, Assam
- ✓ Shri Lakshmi Temple,East Gota Nagar, Fatasil Hills, Guwahati, Assam
- ✓ Dihjari Lakshmi Mandir,Dihjari, Assam
- ✓ Kawaimari Lakshmi Mandir,Kawaimari, Assam
- ✓ Teteliguri Lakshmi Mandir,Kalakuchi, Assam
- ✓ Keotkuchi Lakshmi Mandir Barpeta,Major Gaon, Assam
- ✓ Lakshmi Mandir,Majkuchi, Assam
- ✓ Jayanti Shaktipeeth Shri Nartiang Durga Temple, Nartiang, Meghalaya
- ✓ ISKCON Temple, Imphal,Manipur
- ✓ Shri Laxmi Narayan Mandir,Tidim Rd, New Colony, Loktak, Manipur

Lakshmi Temples In Punjab

- ✓ Shree Mahalakshmi Mandir,Jail Rd, Near Natha Bagichi Mandir, Adarsh Nagar, Jalandhar
- ✓ Shri Laxmi Narayan Mandir,Sultanpur Lodhi Rd, A Block, Near, Model House, Jalandhar
- ✓ Laxmi Narayan Mandir,Guru Nanak Pura,

Amritsar

- ✓ Lakshmi Narayan Mandir,Phase 5, Sector 59, Sahibzada Ajit Singh Nagar
- ✓ Shri Laxmi Narayan Mandir, Model Town, Pathankot
- ✓ Shri Lakshmi Narayan Mandir,Sector-2, Talwara Twp
- ✓ Lakshmi Narayan Mandir,Civil Lines, Patiala
- ✓ Laxmi Narayan Mandir,New Deep Nagar, Civil Lines, Ludhiana

Lakshmi Temples In Kashmir

- ✓ Maha Lakshmi Temple, Pacca Danga, Pakki Dhaki, Old Heritage City, Jammu
- ✓ Lakshmi Narayan Temple, Bhaderwah
- ✓ Shri Laxmi Narayan Temple,Gandhi Nagar, Jammu

Lakshmi Temples In Gujrat

- ✓ Vaibhav Laxmi Mandir,Gordhanwadi no tekro, Chattrabhuj Colony, Pushpkunj, Maninagar, Ahmedabad
- ✓ Laxmi Narayan Mandir,Uttar Gujrat Patel Society Rd, Jahangirpura, Asarwa, Ahmedabad
- ✓ Panchdev Mandir and Vaibhav Laxmi Dham,Nilmani Society, Memnagar, Ahmedabad
- ✓ Shree Laxmi Narayan Mandir,Usmanpura, Ahmedabad

- ✓ Maha Laxmi Temple,Anand Mahal Rd, Chatrapati Shivaji Nagar, Adajan Gam, Adajan, Surat
- ✓ Mahalakshmi Temple,Sultanabad, Dumas, Surat
- ✓ Maa Lakshmi Mandir,Dr Babasaheb Ambedkar Rd, Bakrawadi, Navapura, Vadodara
- ✓ Laxmi Temple,Sardar Ganj, Patan
- ✓ Manilaxmi Jain Tirth, NH 8, near Big Canal, Manej

Lakshmi Temples In Himachal

- ✓ Laxmi Narayan Temple,NH 22, Housing Board Colony, Sanjauli, Shimla
- ✓ Shri Laxmi Narayan Mandir ,Shankli, Longwood, Shimla
- ✓ Laxmi Narayan Mandir,Excise Colony, Bilaspur
- ✓ Chaurasi Temple,Bharmour (60 kilometers from Chamba Valley)
- ✓ Laxmi Narayana Temple,Mohalla, Hatnala Gali, Chamba

◆ ◆ ◆

THANKS

I hope you found this puja book useful!
So start sacred mantra chanting of Maa Lakshmi regularly and remove all your obstacles in life!
Please do share your experience and suggestions as a review in Amazon's Kindle store to appreciate my efforts. It will motivate me to write more. Once again, thank you for downloading and reading this book.

- Santhi Sivakumar

Made in the USA
Coppell, TX
10 April 2024

31153461R00049